The YO
MOSES

illustrated by Leon Baxter
adapted by Diana Craig

Macdonald

In one small corner of Egypt, just where the great river Nile runs into the sea, there lived some people called Israelites. They had come to Egypt many years before to look for food, because all their own crops had died.

God had promised to look after the Israelites in their new home, and at first everyone was very happy. There was plenty to eat, and they grew strong and had lots of children. Soon their families filled the land.

But then everything changed. The king of Egypt, who was called the Pharaoh, died, and a new Pharaoh became king. He hated the Israelites.

'There are so many of them,' he grumbled. 'Just think what would happen if they turned against us. They might even take sides with our enemies. We must stop them!'

So he thought of a plan. 'We'll make them our slaves,' he announced with an evil grin. 'We'll work them so hard they won't even have time to think of fighting us . . . with a bit of luck they may even die of exhaustion!'

So the Israelites slaved from sunrise to sunset, making bricks and moving huge stones to build Egyptian cities. When they were not building cities, they had to dig the fields and plant all the wheat and barley.

The Israelites were exhausted, just as the Pharaoh had hoped. But they didn't die. In fact, they didn't even get ill. They stayed just as strong and healthy as ever. The Pharaoh's wicked plan wasn't working.

So he had another idea. He told the nurses that they must kill all Israelite baby boys as soon as they were born. But the nurses knew that God would punish them if they did such a terrible thing, so they made up an excuse.

'We're so sorry, Your Majesty,' they lied, not daring to look the Pharaoh in the eye. 'But the babies are born so quickly that we never get there in time.'

'All right then,' replied the Pharaoh angrily. 'They'll just have to be thrown in the river instead!'

All the Israelite mothers were terrified, and tried to hide their babies. One mother hid her newborn boy in a corner of her house. If anyone heard him crying and wondered about the noise, she knew exactly what to say.

'It's a sick sheep I'm looking after,' she would tell them. 'Funny, isn't it, how they sound just like babies when they're ill?' No one suspected anything.

But soon the baby grew too big to hide. 'I know what I'll do,' thought his mother. 'I'll put him in a basket on the river, near where the Pharaoh's daughter comes to wash every morning, and she's sure to find him. She has no children of her own, and she's not nearly as cruel as that wicked king. Perhaps she'll feel sorry for my baby and save him.'

So the mother took a big basket and painted the outside with black, sticky stuff called pitch, to stop the water getting in. Then she laid the baby inside and put the basket among the reeds near the river bank. She told her daughter, Miriam, to stay and see what happened.

Sure enough, the princess came down to the water's edge and spotted the basket. She sent one of her servants to fetch it, and she was amazed to see a little baby tucked up snugly inside.

'Whatever are you doing here?' she exclaimed, picking him up and giving him a cuddle. And then she guessed the truth.

'You must be one of the Israelite babies, and your mother has hidden you here for safety. Well, I don't care what my father says. *I* won't throw you in the river.'

Miriam crept out of her hiding place. 'Er, excuse me, Your Royal Highness,' she began, nervously. 'But would Your Highness like me to find someone to look after that baby?'

'Yes, as a matter of fact I would. I'm much too busy to do it myself,' replied the princess, who knew nothing about babies.

'Oh, I'll pay the woman, of course,' she added.

Miriam rushed off to tell her own mother, who was overjoyed. Not only was her baby safe, but she was going to look after him herself — and get paid for doing it, too!

When the little boy was old enough, his mother took him back to the princess. 'From now on, I shall be his mother,' the princess said, 'and I'll call him Moses, which means "taken from the water".' So Moses was brought up like an Egyptian prince, and had everything he could wish for.

But as the years went by, one thing began to bother Moses more and more. Although he lived with the Egyptians, he knew he wasn't one of them. He knew he was really an Israelite. He saw how cruel the Egyptians were to his people and it made him very angry. How could the Egyptians treat them so badly? They hadn't done anything wrong. It just wasn't fair.

One day, when Moses had grown up, he decided to visit one of the building sites and see for himself what was going on. He caught sight of one of the Egyptian slave drivers beating an Israelite slave. Moses completely lost his temper. He picked up a stone and smashed it on the slave driver's head. The man fell to the ground, dead. Moses was horrified at what he had done. Quickly, he buried the body in the sand.

'Don't breathe a word of what's happened, or the Pharaoh will have me killed!' he warned the slave. But the man just couldn't help telling his brother, and his brother told his aunt, and his aunt told her friend . . . and soon everyone knew.

The next day, Moses visited another building site, and saw a big, strong slave bullying a small, weak slave.

'Stop that, you great bully!' shouted Moses.

'Just you try and make me!' the slave answered back cheekily. 'You can't boss me about, or I'll tell the Pharaoh how you killed one of his men!'

Moses was terrified. His secret was out, and he knew that when the Pharaoh heard, that would be the end of him.

So, that night, he packed a few clothes and some food and, with a last, longing look at his home, he crept away.

Moses walked on and on, out into the desert, until Egypt was far behind. At last he came to a well and stopped to rest.

He had almost dozed off when, suddenly, he was startled by the sound of angry voices shouting. Some shepherd girls had come to the well to get water for their sheep, but some other shepherds were chasing them away.

Wearily, Moses pulled himself to his feet.

'Why don't you share the water?' he asked the shepherds. 'There's plenty for everyone.'

The shepherds agreed, grudgingly, and Moses helped the girls give water to their sheep.

The girls went home and told their father about Moses. The old man was amazed. 'Don't tell me you left him out there in the desert, after all his trouble!' he cried. 'Where are your manners? Go and fetch him at once!'

The old man invited Moses to stay with his family. Much later, Moses married one of the girls and they had two sons. Moses settled down to a quiet life, looking after the sheep. He had to work very hard. He no longer slept on a soft golden bed in the royal palace, but on the hard ground inside a tent. It was all very different from his life in Egypt, but slowly he got used to it. At least he was safe.

Meanwhile, back in Egypt, things were getting worse and worse for the Israelites. God saw how unhappy they were, and he knew it was time to keep the promise he had made to look after them.

'I must think of a way for them to escape from Egypt,' he thought. 'But they'll need someone to lead them. I wonder who could do that . . . ?' And then God remembered Moses.

As usual, Moses was in the desert, looking after the sheep. Clumps of withered grass and dry bushes grew all around him, in the hot, dusty earth. Suddenly, he noticed that one of the bushes was on fire.

He was just about to take a closer look, to see if the fire was dangerous, when he realised that there was something very strange about it. The bush was certainly ablaze with flames, but the branches weren't black and the leaves weren't shrivelled. Could it be true? The bush was on fire, but it wasn't burning!

Then Moses heard God's voice, coming from the middle of the flames. 'Go back to Egypt,' God said. 'Speak to the Pharaoh. Tell him that the Israelites must have three days off work so they can go into the desert to hold a festival and pray to me. But as soon as he lets them go, tell them never to go back to Egypt.'

'Oh, no!' thought Moses. 'Why me? Of course I feel sorry for the Israelites, but the Pharaoh frightens me! I'd much rather stay here and look after the sheep.'

So Moses thought of an excuse. 'Thank you for asking me, G-God,' he stammered nervously, 'but really I'm not b-brave enough for such an important job.'

'Never mind. I'll be with you,' said God.

'But no one will believe you sent me,' Moses protested.

'I'll show you how to prove it,' said God. He showed Moses how, if he threw his shepherd's staff on to the ground, it could turn into a snake.

'And if that doesn't convince them,' God added, 'just pour some river water on to the ground and it will turn into blood. That should make them believe you!'

Moses was getting desperate. 'But I could never persuade the Pharaoh!' he wailed. 'I s-stutter when I'm s-scared . . .'

God began to lose his patience. 'All right, then,' he said. 'I'll send your brother Aaron with you. He's a good talker. Now, off you go, and no more excuses.'

Moses could see that there was no point in arguing. God had made his decision, and that was that!

'Don't worry,' God called, as Moses gathered his sheep together. 'The old Pharaoh is dead now. There's a new one on the throne. He doesn't know you once killed an Egyptian.' That was a relief!

Moses went home and said good-bye to his friends. Then, with his wife and sons by his side, he set off for Egypt.

When they came to the place where Moses had seen the burning bush, Aaron was waiting for them. Moses rushed up to him in delight, and threw his arms around his neck. He told him everything God had said.

‘At first the Pharaoh won’t listen to us,’ Moses said. ‘But God will punish him so badly, and all his people, that in the end he will beg us to go.’

After talking to Aaron, Moses began to feel better. He knew that the job would not be easy, but it was what God wanted. In the end, they would succeed.

So Moses, his wife and children, and Aaron all set off for Egypt. They weren’t sure what lay in store for them, but they knew that this was the most important journey of their lives. They were going to set the Israelites free from slavery for ever.

This story has been told in many different ways for more than three thousand years. It was first written down in a language called Hebrew. Since then, it has been re-told in almost every language used in the world today.

You can find the story of Moses in the Bible. This part of his life is in the Book of Exodus, Chapters 1 to 4.

There is a companion to this book called 'Moses and the Flight from Egypt'. It tells the story of Moses' struggles in Egypt and how he finally rescued the Israelites.